TIN PAN ALLEY

5 CLASSICS ARRANGED WITH A TOUCH OF JAZZ BY PHILLIP KEVEREN

— PIANO LEVEL —
INTERMEDIATE

ISBN 978-1-5400-3134-1

Visit Hal Leonard Online at
www.halleonard.com

Visit Phillip at
www.phillipkeveren.com

Contact Us:
Hal Leonard
7777 West Bluemound Road
Milwaukee, WI 53213
Email: info@halleonard.com

In Europe contact:
Hal Leonard Europe Limited
Distribution Centre, Newmarket Road
Bury St Edmunds, Suffolk, IP33 3YB
Email: info@halleonardeurope.com

In Australia contact:
Hal Leonard Australia Pty. Ltd.
4 Lentara Court
Cheltenham, Victoria, 3192 Australia
Email: info@halleonard.com.au

PREFACE

The New York City music publishers and songwriters who dominated the American popular music scene in the late 1880s and early 1900s are often collectively called "Tin Pan Alley." The moniker is thought to be a reference to the din of many pianos being played simultaneously – comparing them to the clanging of tin pans!

This collection of golden tunes has been arranged with a touch of jazz. That is not a huge stretch, of course, as these popular songs were written during the time when jazz was also emerging in the United States.

Writing this book was a lot of fun. I hope you enjoying playing these settings!

Sincerely,

Phillip Keveren

BIOGRAPHY

Phillip Keveren, a multi-talented keyboard artist and composer, has composed original works in a variety of genres from piano solo to symphonic orchestra. Mr. Keveren gives frequent concerts and workshops for teachers and their students in the United States, Canada, Europe, and Asia. Mr. Keveren holds a B.M. in composition from California State University Northridge and a M.M. in composition from the University of Southern California.

CONTENTS

BY THE LIGHT
OF THE SILVERY MOON

Lyric by ED MADDEN
Music by GUS EDWARDS
Arranged by Phillip Keveren

6

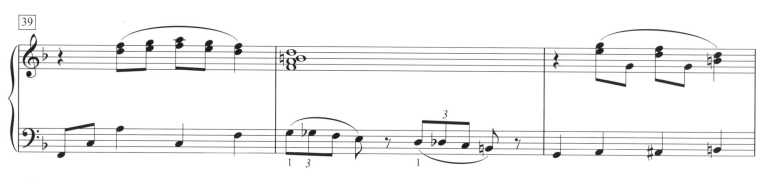

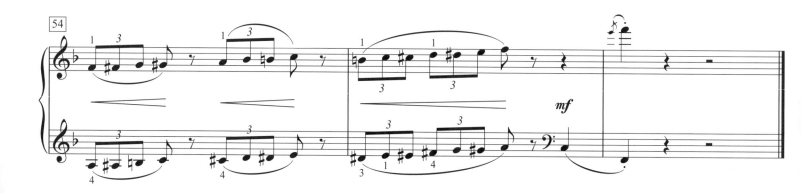

CAROLINA IN THE MORNING

Lyrics by GUS KAHN
Music by WALTER DONALDSON
Arranged by Phillip Keveren

THE DARKTOWN STRUTTERS' BALL
from THE STORY OF VERNON AND IRENE CASTLE

Words and Music by
SHELTON BROOKS
Arranged by Phillip Keveren

Steady jazz (♩ = 144)

FOR ME AND MY GAL

Words by EDGAR LESLIE and E. RAY GOETZ
Music by GEORGE W. MEYER
Arranged by Phillip Keveren

Jazz Ballad, with rubato ($\quarternote$ = c. 116)

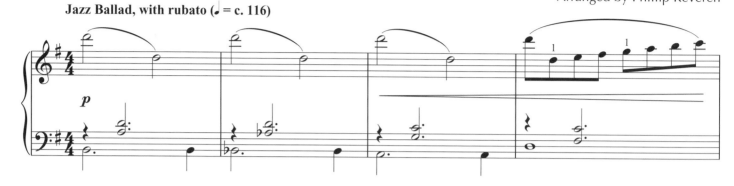

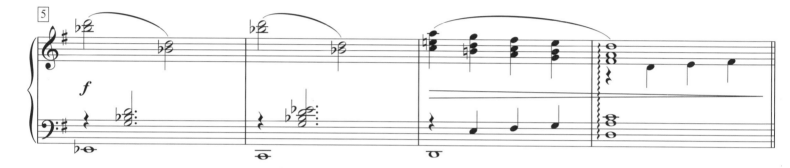

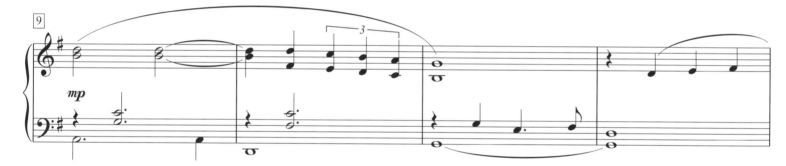

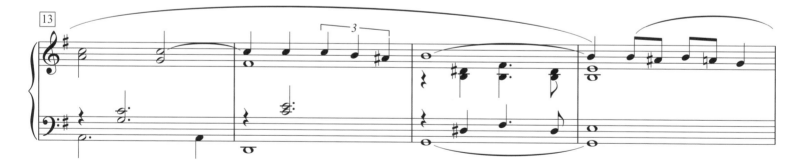

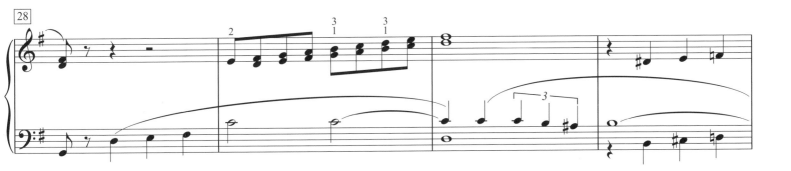

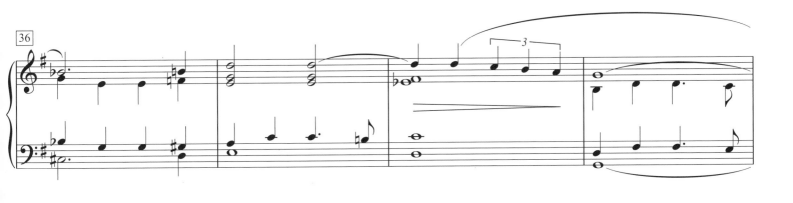

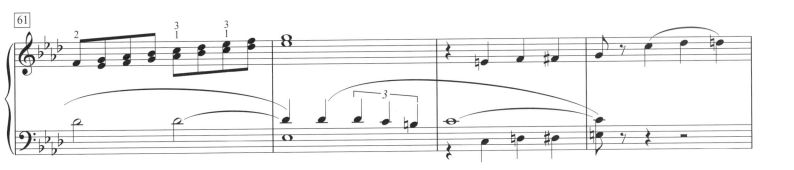

GIVE MY REGARDS TO BROADWAY

from LITTLE JOHNNY JONES

Words and Music by
GEORGE M. COHAN
Arranged by Phillip Keveren

Showtime fast (♩ = 126-132)

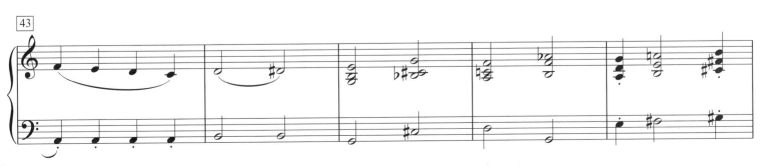

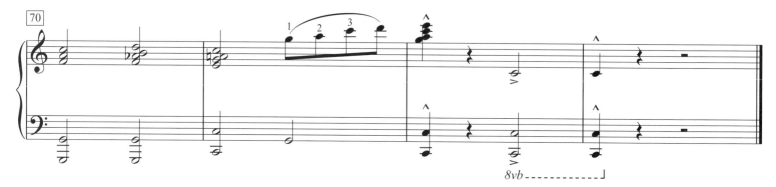

LET ME CALL YOU SWEETHEART

Words by BETH SLATER WHITSON
Music by LEO FRIEDMAN
Arranged by Phillip Keveren

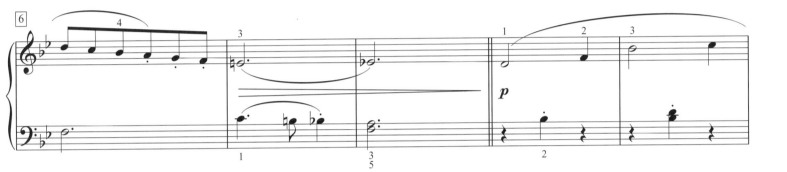

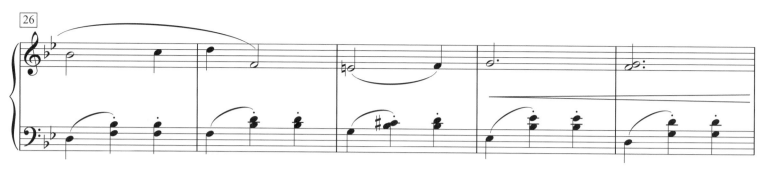

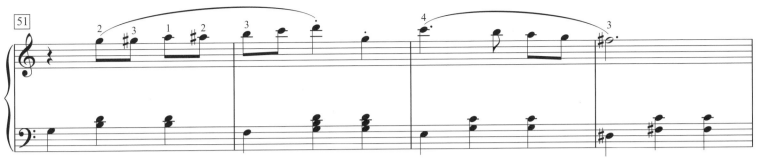

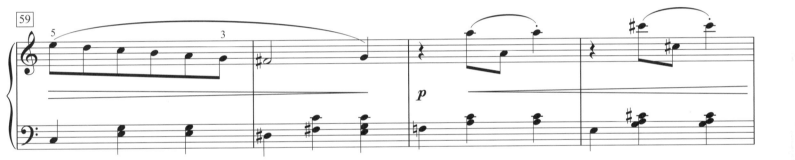

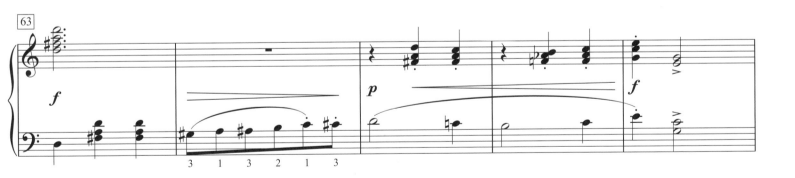

INDIANA
(Back Home Again in Indiana)

Words by BALLARD MacDONALD
Music by JAMES F. HANLEY
Arranged by Phillip Keveren

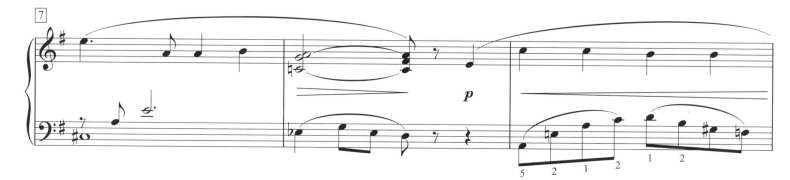

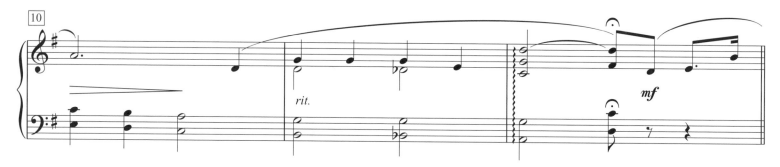

MY MELANCHOLY BABY

Words by GEORGE NORTON
Music by ERNIE BURNETT
Arranged by Phillip Keveren

Tender Ballad, with rubato (♩ = c. 116)

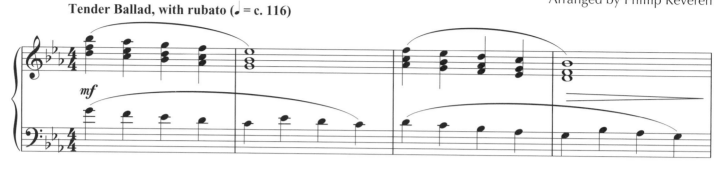

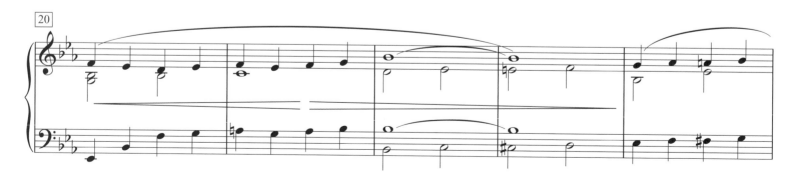

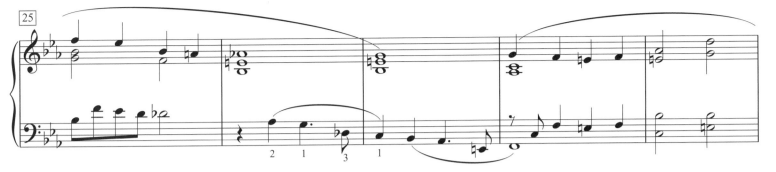

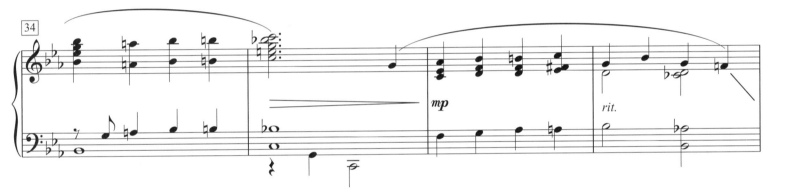

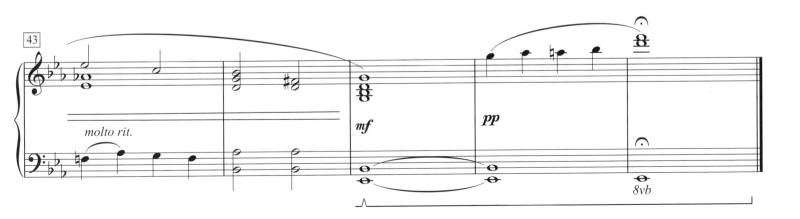

ROCK-A-BYE YOUR BABY
WITH A DIXIE MELODY

from SINBAD

Words by SAM M. LEWIS
and JOE YOUNG
Music by JEAN SCHWARTZ
Arranged by Phillip Keveren

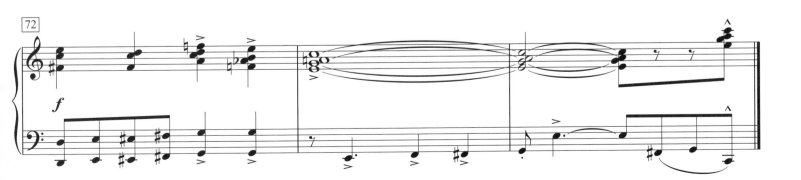

SECOND HAND ROSE

Words by GRANT CLARKE
Music by JAMES F. HANLEY
Arranged by Phillip Keveren

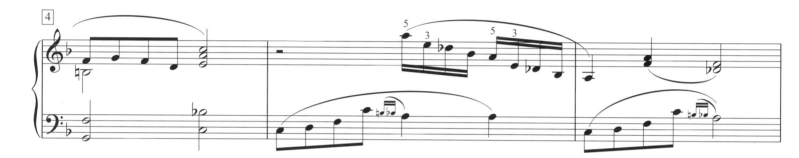

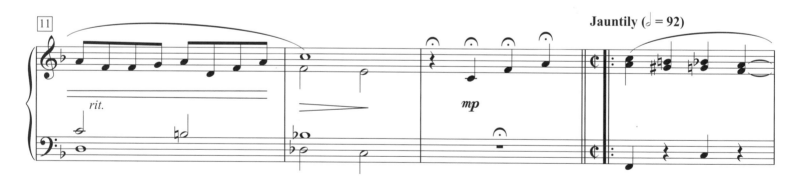

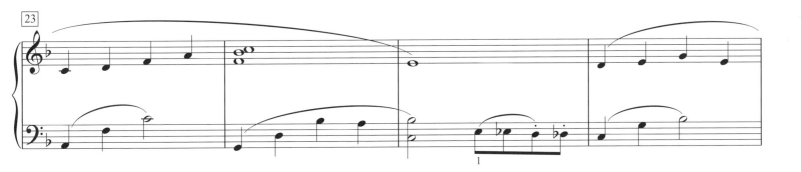

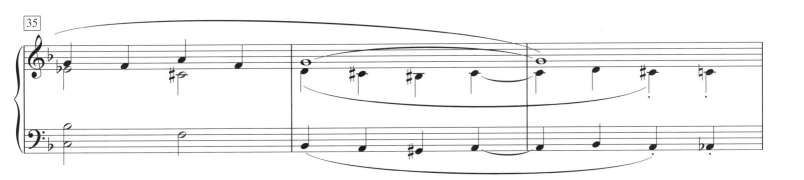

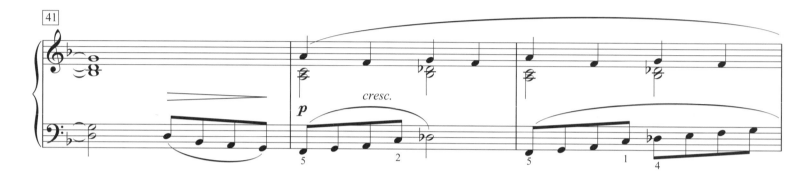

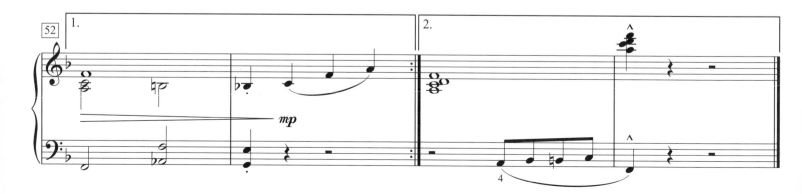

TAKE ME OUT TO THE BALL GAME

Words by JACK NORWORTH
Music by ALBERT VON TILZER
Arranged by Phillip Keveren

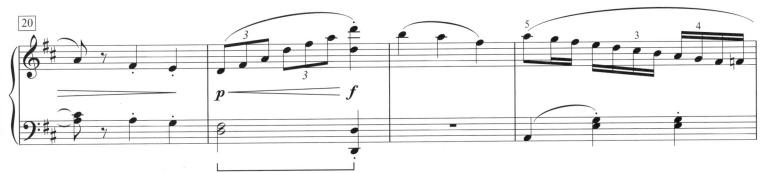

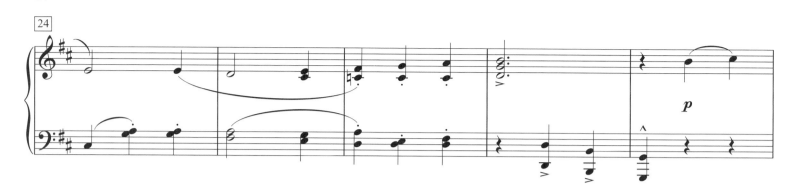

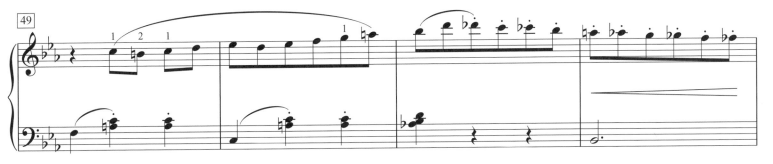

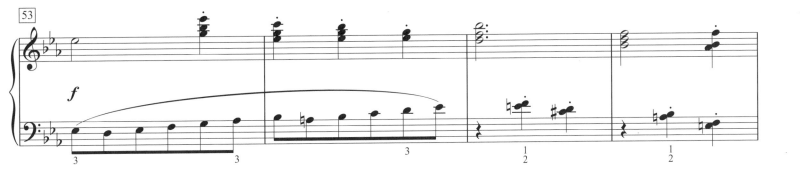

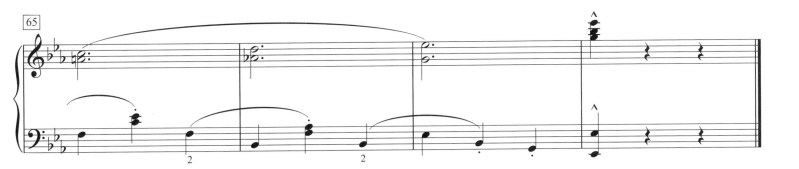

SHINE ON, HARVEST MOON

Words by JACK NORWORTH
Music by NORA BAYES
and JACK NORWORTH
Arranged by Phillip Keveren

Moderately slow, with rubato (♩ = c. 96)

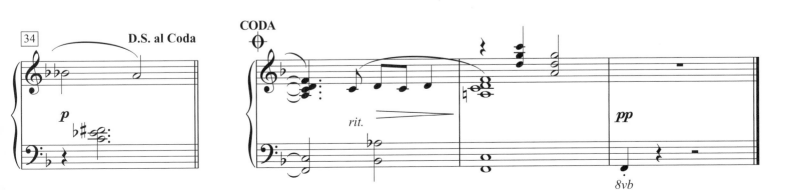

TOOT, TOOT, TOOTSIE!
(Good-bye!)
from THE JAZZ SINGER

Words and Music by GUS KAHN,
ERNIE ERDMAN, DAN RUSSO and TED FIORITO
Arranged by Phillip Keveren

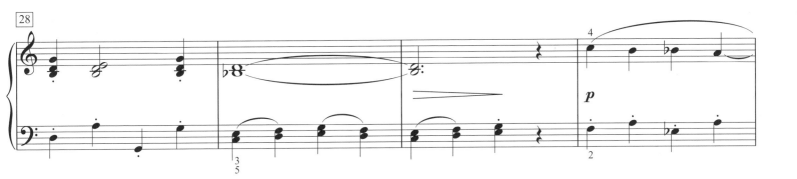

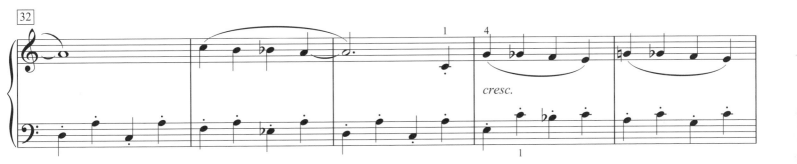

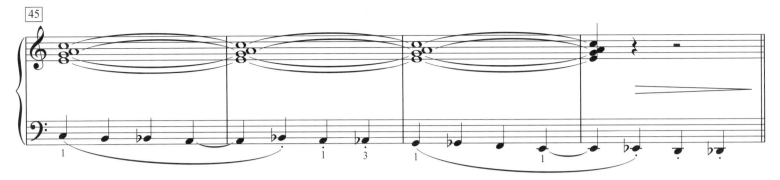

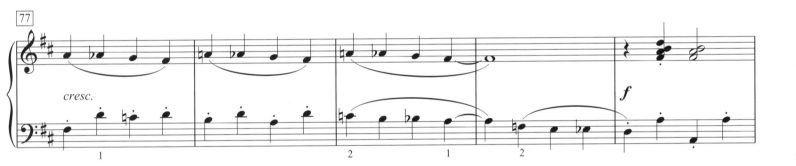

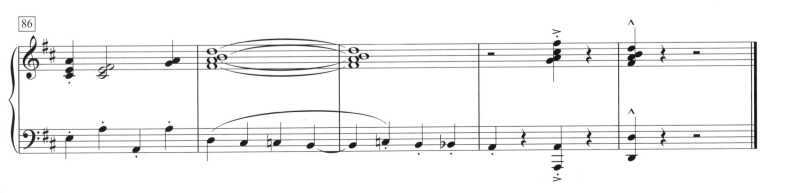

TWELFTH STREET RAG

By EUDAY L. BOWMAN
Arranged by Phillip Keveren

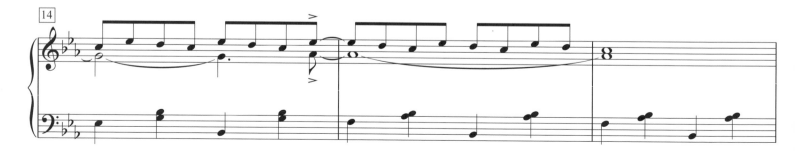

YOU MADE ME LOVE YOU
(I Didn't Want to Do It)
from BROADWAY MELODY OF 1938

Words by JOE McCARTHY
Music by JAMES V. MONACO
Arranged by Phillip Keveren

Ballad, with freedom (♩ = c. 88)

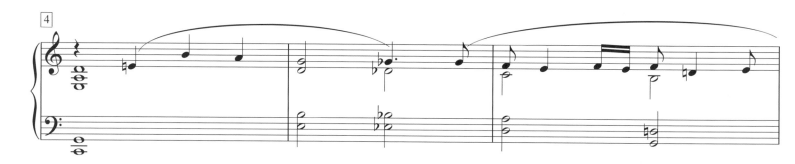

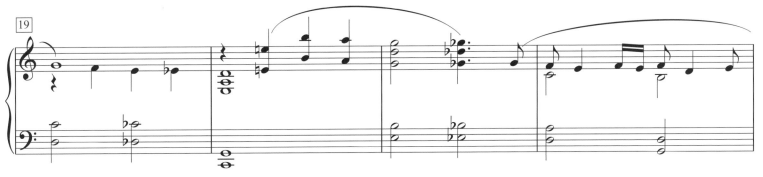

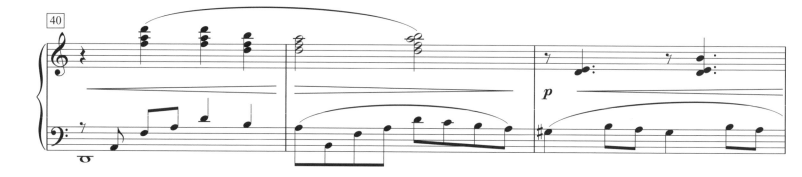